No XXXV

THE MINOR DRAMA.

BOMBASTES FURIOSO,

A Burlesque Tragic Opera,

IN ONE ACT

BY THOMAS BARNES RHODES.

WITH THE STAGE BUSINESS, CAST OF CHARACTERS, COSTUMES, RELATIVE POSITIONS ETC.

NEW YORK:
SAMUEL FRENCH & SON,
PUBLISHERS,
28 WEST 23D STREET.

LONDON:
SAMUEL FRENCH.
PUBLISHER,
89 STRAND.

SCENERY.

With a view to obviate the great difficulty experienced by Amateurs (particularly in country houses) in obtaining Scenery, &c., to fix in a Drawing Room, and then only by considerable outlay for hire and great damage caused to walls, we have decided to keep a series of Scenes, &c., coloured on strong paper, which can be joined together or pasted on canvas or wood, according to requirements. Full directions, with diagrams shewing exact size of Back Scenes, Borders, and Wings, can be had free on application. The following four scenes each consists of thirty sheets of paper.

GARDEN.

The above is an illustration of this scene. It is kept in two sizes. The small size would extend to 15 feet wide and 8 feet high, and the large size to 20 feet long and 11½ feet high. It is not necessary to have the scene the height of the room, as blue paper to represent sky is usually hung at the top. Small size, with Wings and Border complete, $7.50; large size, do., **$10.00.**

WOOD.

This is similar in style to the above, only a wood scene is introduced in the centre. It is kept in two sizes, as the previous scene, and blue paper can introduced as before indicated. Small size, with Wings and Borders complete, $7 50; large size, do., $10.00.

FOLIAGE.—This is a sheet of paper on which foliage is drawn, which can be repeated and cut in any shape required. Small size, 30 in. by 20 in., 25 cts. per sheet; large size, 40 in. by 30 in., 35 cts. per sheet.

DRAWING ROOM.

This scene is only kept in the large size, to extend to 20 feet long and 11½ feet high. In the centre is a French window, leading down to the ground, which could be made practicable if required. On the left wing is a fire-place with mirror above, and on the right wing is an oil painting. The whole scene is tastefully ornamented and beautifully coloured, forming a most elegant picture. Should a box scene be required extra wings can be had, consisting of doors each side, which could be made practicable. Price, with Border and one set of Wings, $10.; with Border and two sets of Wings, to form box scene, $12.50.

COTTAGE INTERIOR.

This is also kept in the large size only. In the centre is a door leading outside. On the left centre is a rustic fireplace, and the right centre is a window. On the wings are painted shelves, &c., to complete the scene. A box scene can be made by purchasing extra wings, as before described, and forming doors on each side. Price, with Border and one set of Wings, $10.00; with Border and two sets of Wings, to form box scene, $12.50.

The Drawing Room mounted can be seen at 28 West 23d St., New York. Full directions accompany each Scene.

THE MINOR DRAMA

No. XXXV

BOMBASTES FURIOSO

A Burlesque Tragic Opera,

IN ONE ACT.

BY THOMAS BARNES RHODES.

WITH THE STAGE BUSINESS, CAST OF CHARACTERS, COSTUMES, RELATIVE POSITIONS, ETC.

New York:
SAMUEL FRENCH & SON,
PUBLISHERS,
28 WEST 23D STREET.

London:
SAMUEL FRENCH,
PUBLISHER,
89, STRAND.

BOMBASTES FURIOSO

ACT I.

Scene I.—*Interior of the Palace.*

Artaxominous *in his Chair of State.—A Table, set out with bowls, glasses, pipes, &c.—Attendants on each side.*

TRIO.

Air—"*Tekeli.*"

1st Att. What will your Majesty please to wear?
Or blue, green, red, black, white, or brown?
2d Att. D'ye choose to look at the bill of fare?
Art. Get out of my sight, or I'll knock you down.
2d Att. Here is soup, fish, or goose, or duck, or fowl or pigeons, pig, or hare;
1st Att. Blue, green, or red, or black, white, or brown,
What will your Majesty, &c.
Art. Get out of my sight, &c.

[*Exeunt Attendants,* R. *and* L.

Enter Fusbos, L., *and kneels to the King.*

Fus. Hail, Artaxominous! ycleped the Great!
I come, an humble pillar of thy state,
Pregnant with news—but ere that news I tell,
First let me hope your Majesty is well.
Art. Rise, learnéd Fusbos! rise, my friend, and know,
We are but middling—that is, but *so so.*
Fus. Only *so so!* Oh, monstrous, doleful thing!
Is it the mulligrubs affects the king?
Or, dropping poisons in the cup of joy,
Do the blue devils your repose annoy?

Art. Nor mulligrubs, nor devils blue are here,
But yet we feel ourself a little *queer.*
Fus. Yes, I perceive it in that vacant eye,
The vest unbuttoned, and the wig awry:
So sickly cats neglect their fur-attire,
And sit and mope beside the kitchen fire.
Art. Last night, when undisturbed by state affairs,
Moist'ning our clay, and puffing off our cares,
Oft the replenished goblet did we drain,
And drank, and smoked, and smoked and drank again;
Such was the case, our very actions such,
Until at length we got a drop too much.
Fus. So, when some donkey on the Blackheath road
Falls, overpowered, beneath his sandy load,
The driver's curse unheeded swells the air,
Since none can carry more than they can bear.
Art. The sapient Doctor Muggins came in haste,
Who suits his physic to his patients' taste;
He, knowing well on what our heart is set,
Hath just prescribed "to take a morning whet;"
The very sight each sick'ning pain subdues,
Then sit, my Fusbos, sit, and tell thy news.
Fus. [*Sits* L. *of table.*] Gen'ral Bombastes, whose resistless force
Alone exceeds by far a brewer's horse,
Returns victorious, bringing mines of wealth!
Art. Does he? by jingo! then we'll drink his health.
[*Drum and fife,* R.
Fus. But hark! with loud acclaim, the fife and drum
Announce your army near; behold, they come!
[*Drum and fife again,* R.

Enter BOMBASTES, R., *attended by one Drummer, one Fifer, and two Soldiers, all very materially differing in size.*

Bom. [*To Army.*] Meet me this ev'ning at the Barley-Mow;
I'll bring your pay, you see I'm busy now:
Begone, brave army, and don't kick up a row.
[*Exeunt Soldiers,* R.
To the King.] Thrashed are your foes—this watch and silken string,
Worn by their chief, I as a trophy bring;

CAST OF CHARACTERS.

	Covent Garden, 1830.	*Park*, [illegible]
Artaxominous	Mr. Mathews.	Mr. H. Placide.
Fusbos	" Taylor.	" Nickinson.
Bombastes.	" Liston.	" J. Fisher.
Distaffina	Mrs. Liston.	Mrs. Vernon.

Attendants, Drummer, Fifer, and two or three Soldiers of different sizes

COSTUMES.

ARTAXOMINOUS, *King of Utopia.*—Full dress court suit, powdered wig

FUSBOS, *Minister of State.*—The same.

GENERAL BOMBASTES.—A general's military suit. Jack boots, comic powdered wig and pigtail, sword and sash, general's hat and plume. *Second dress* Morning gown and slippers.

ATTENDANTS.—Full dress court suits

ARMY.—A long drummer, a short fifer, and two or three soldiers of different dimensions, all dressed in caricature.

DISTAFFINA.—Colored chintz gown, open in front, crimson balimanco petticoat white muslin apron, mob-cap, white muslin handkerchief.

EXITS AND ENTRANCES.

R. means *Right;* L. *Left;* R. D. *Right Door;* L. D. *Left Door;* S. E. *Second Entrance;* U. E. *Upper Entrance;* M. D. *Middle Door.*

RELATIVE POSITIONS.

R. means *Right;* L. *Left;* C. *Centre;* R. C. *Right of Centre;* L. C. *Left of Centre.*

I knocked him down, then snatched it from his fob;
"Watch, watch!" he cried, when I had done the job;
"My watch is gone," says he—says I, "Just so;
Stop where you are—watches were made to go."

Art. For which we make you Duke of Strombelo.

[*Bombastes kneels—the King dubs him with a pipe, and then presents the bowl.*

From our own bowl here drink, my soldier true;
And if you'd like to take a whiff or two,
He whose brave arm hath made our foes to crouch,
Shall have a pipe from this, our royal pouch.

Bom. [*Rises.*] Honors so great have all my toils repaid
My liege, and Fusbos, here's "Success to trade."

Fus. Well said, Bombastes! since thy mighty blows
Have given a quietus to our foes,
Now shall our farmers gather in their crops,
And busy tradesmen mind their crowded shops;
The deadly havoc of war's hatchet cease;
Now shall we smoke the calumet of peace.

Art. I shall smoke short-cut, you smoke what you please

Bom. Whate'er your majesty shall deign to name,
Short cut or *long* to me is all the same.

Bom. & Fus. In short, so long as we your favors claim,
Short cut or *long* to us is all the same.

Art. Thanks, gen'rous friends! now list whilst I impart
How firm you're locked and bolted in my heart:
So long as this here pouch a pipe contains,
Or a full glass in that there bowl remains,
To you an equal portion shall belong;
This I do swear, and now—let's have a song.

Fus. My liege shall be obeyed.

[*Advances and attempts to sing.*

Bom. Fusbos, give place,
You know you haven't got a singing face;
Here nature, smiling, gave the winning grace.

SONG.—Bombastes.

Air—"*Hope told a flatt'ring Tale.*"

Hope told a flattering tale,
Much longer than my arm,
That love and pots of ale,
In peace would keep me warm;

The flatt'rer is not gone,
She visits number one:
In love I'm monstrous deep;
Love! odds bobs, destroys my sleep.

Hope told a flattering tale,
Lest love should soon grow cool;
A tub thrown to a whale,
To make the fish a fool:
Should Distaffina frown,
Then love's gone out of town,
And when love's dream is o'er,
Then we wake and dream no more. [*Exit*, L.

[*The King evinces strong emotions during the song, and at the conclusion starts up.*

Fus. What ails my liege? ah! why that look so sad?
Art. [*Coming forward.*] I am in love! I scorch, I freeze, I'm mad!
Oh, tell me, Fusbos, first and best of friends,
You who have wisdom at your fingers' ends,
Shall it be so, or shall it not be so?
Shall I my Griskinissa's charms forego,
Compel her to give up the regal chair,
And place the rosy Distaffina there!
In such a case, what course can I pursue?
I love my Queen and Distaffina too.
Fus. And would a king his general supplant?
I can't advise, upon my soul I can't.
Art. So when two feasts, whereat there's naught to pay,
Fall unpropitious on the self-same day
The anxious Cit each invitation views,
And ponders which to take or which refuse;
From this or that to keep away is loth,
And sighs to think he cannot dine at both. [*Exit*, L.
Fus. So when some school-boy, on a rainy day,
Finds all his playmates will no longer stay,
He takes the hint himself—and walks away. [*Exit*, R.

SCENE II.—*Another Apartment in the Palace.*

Enter ARTAXOMINOUS, L.

Art. I'll seek the maid I love, though in my way
A dozen gen'rals stood in fierce array!

Such rosy beauties nature meant for kings;
Subjects have treat enough to see such things

SONG. *

AIR—"*Paddy O'Carroll.*"

My love is so pretty,
So lively and witty,
None in town or city
Her hand would disgrace!
My lord of the woolsack,
His coachman would pull back,
To get a look full smack
At her pretty face.
Mathematical teachers,
Stiff methodist preachers,
And all the gay creatures
That run about town—
Great foreign ambassadors
Never can pass her doors,
But my sweet lass deplores
So much renown. Fal de ral, &c.

Though she drives a wheelbarrow,
Through streets wide and narrow,
The school-boys from Harrow
May laugh if they dare.
Nor tasteful Grassini,
Nor Billingtonini,
Divine Catalina,
With her can compare.
Nor head with a mitre,
Nor Belcher the fighter,
Can find out a brighter
Than my pretty maid.
But my words are mere playthings,
Neat trim holiday-things,
They cannot half say things
Enough for my love. Fal de ral, &c.

She's young and she's tender,
She's tall and she's slender,
As straight as a fender
From the top to the toe.
Eyes like stars glittering,
Mouth always tittering,
Fingers to fit a ring
Ne'er were made so.

* This comic song was not written by the author of the piece.

Her head like a holly-bow'r,
Cheeks like a cauliflower,
Nose like a jolly tower
By the sea-side.
Then haste, oh ye days and nights,
That I may taste delights,
And with church holy rites
Make her my bride. Fal de ral, &c.
[*Exit*, R.

SCENE III.—*Inside of a Cottage.*

Enter DISTAFFINA, R.

Dis. This morn, as sleeping in my bed I lay
I dreamt, (and morning dreams come true, they say,)
I dreamt a cunning man my fortune told,
And soon the pots and pans were turned to gold!
Then I resolved to cut a mighty dash;
But, lo! ere I could turn them into cash,
Another cunning man my heart betrayed,
Stole all away, and left my debts unpaid.

Enter ARTAXOMINOUS, L.

And pray, sir, who are you, I'd wish to know?
Art. Perfection's self, oh, smooth that angry brow!
For love of thee I've wandered through the town,
And here have come to offer half a crown.
Dis. Fellow! your paltry offer I despise;
The great Bombastes' love alone I prize.
Art. He's but a Gen'ral—damsel, I'm a King;
Dis. Oh, sir! that makes it quite another thing.
Art. And think not, maiden, I could e'er design
A sum so trifling for such charms as thine.
No! the half crown that tinged thy cheeks with red,
And bade fierce anger o'er thy beauties spread,
Was meant that thou shouldst share my throne and bed.
Dis. [*Aside.*] My dream is out, and I shall soon behold
The pots and pans all turn to shining gold.
Art. [*Puts his hat down to kneel on.*] Here on my knees
(those knees which ne'er till now
To man or maid in suppliance bent,) I vow
Still to remain, till you my hopes fulfil,
Fixed as the monument on Fish-street hill.

Dis. [*Kneels.*] And thus I swear, as I bestow my hand
As long as e'er the Monument shall stand,
So long I'm yours—

Art. Are then my wishes crowned?

Dis. La, sir! I'd not say no for twenty pound;
Let silly maids for love their favors yield,
Rich ones for me—a king against the field.

SONG.—DISTAFFINA.

AIR—"*Paddy's Wedding.*"

Queen Dido at
Her palace gate
Sat darning of her stocking, O;
She sung and drew
The worsted through,
Whilst her foot was the cradle rocking, O,
(For a babe she had
By a soldier lad,
Though hist'ry passes it over, O;)
"You tell-tale brat,
"I've been a flat,
"Your daddy has proved a rover O.

"What a fool was I
"To be cozened by
"A fellow without a penny, O;
"When rich ones came,
"And asked the same,
"For I'd offers from never so many, O.
"But I'll darn my hose,
"Look out for beaus,
"And quickly get a new lover, O;
"Then come, lads, come,
"Love beats the drum,
"And a fig for Æneas the rover, O."

Art. So Orpheus sung of old, or poets lie,
And as the brutes were charmed, e'en so am I.
Rosy-cheeked maid, henceforth my only queen,
Full soon shalt thou in royal robes be seen;
And through my realms I'll issue this decree,
None shall appear of taller growth than thee;
Painters no other face portray—each sign
O'er ale-house hung shall change its head for thine.
Poets shall cancel their unpublished lays,
And none presume to write but in thy praise.

Dis. [*Produces a bottle and glass,* R.] And may I then, without offending, crave
My love to taste of this, the best I have?

Art. Were it the vilest liquor upon earth,
Thy touch would render it of matchless worth.
Dear shall the gift be held that comes from you;
Best proof of love—[*Drinks.*]—'tis full proof Hodges' too!
Through all my veins I feel a genial glow,
It fires my soul—

Bom. [*Within,* L.] Ho, Distaffina, ho!

Art. Heard you that voice?

Dis. Oh, yes; 'tis what's-his-name,
The General; send him packing as he came.

Art. And is it he? and doth he hither come?
Ah, me! my guilty conscience strikes me dumb,
Where shall I go? say, whither shall I fly?
Hide me, oh, hide me from his injured eye!

Dis. Why, sure, you're not alarmed at such a thing!
He's but a General, and you're a King.

[*Artaxominous secretes himself in a closet,* R.

Enter BOMBASTES, L.

Bom. Loved Distaffina! now by my scars I vow,
Scars got—I haven't time to tell you how;
By all the risks my fearless heart hath run,
Risks of all shapes from bludgeon, sword, and gun,
Steel traps, the patrole, bailiff shrewd, and dun;
By the great bunch of laurels on my brow,
Ne'er did thy charms exceed their present glow!
Oh, let me greet thee with a loving kiss— [*Sees the hat*
Hell and the devil! say whose hat is this?

Dis. Why, help your silly brains, that's not a hat.

Bom. No hat?

Dis. Suppose it is, why what of that?
A hat can do no harm without a head!

Bom. Whoe'er it fits, this hour I doom him dead;
Alive from hence the caitiff shall not stir—

[*Discovers the King*

Your most obedient, humble servant, sir.

Art. Oh, General, oh!

Bom. My much loved master, oh!
What means all this?

Art. Indeed, I hardly know—

Dis. (R.) You hardly know!—a very pretty joke,
If kingly promises so soon are broke!
Arn't I to be a queen, and dress so fine?

Art. (L.) I do repent me of the foul design;
To thee, my brave Bombastes, I restore.
Pure Distaffina, and will never more
Through lane or street with lawless passion rove,
But give to Griskinissa all my love.

Bom. (C.) No, no; I'll love no more: let him who can
Fancy the maid who fancies ev'ry man.
In some lone place I'll find a gloomy cave,
There my own hands shall dig a spacious grave
Then all unseen I'll lay me down and die,
Since woman's constancy is—all my eye.

TRIO.

AIR—"*Oh, lady fair.*"

Dis. Oh, cruel man, where are you going?
Sad are my wants, my rent is owing.
Bom. I go, I go, all comfort scorning;
Some death I'll die before the morning
Dis. Heigho, heigho, sad is that warning;
Oh, do not die before the morning.
Art. I'll follow him, all danger scorning;
He shall not die before the morning.
Bom. I go, I go, &c.
Dis. Heigho, heigho, &c.
Art. I'll follow him, &c. [*Exeunt*, L.

SCENE IV.—*A Wood.*

Enter FUSBOS.

Fus. This day is big with fate; just as I set
My foot across the threshold, lo! I met
A man, whose squint terrific struck my view;
Another came, and, lo! he squinted too;
And ere I reached the corner of the street,
Some ten short paces, 'twas my lot to meet
A third who squinted more—a fourth, and he
Squinted more vilely than the other three.

Such omens met the eye when Cæsar fell,
But cautioned him in vain; and who can tell
Whether those awful notices of fate
Are meant for kings, or ministers of state?
For rich or poor, old, young, or short or tall,
The wrestler Love trips up the heels of all.

SONG.

AIR—"*My Lodging is on the cold Ground.*"

My lodging is in Leather-lane,
A parlor that's next to the sky;
'Tis exposed to the wind and the rain,
But the wind and the rain I defy:
Such love warms the coldest of spots,
As I feel for Scrubinda the fair;
Oh, she lives by the scouring of pots,
In Dyott-street, Bloomsbury-square.

Oh, was I a quart, pint, or gill,
To be scrubbed by her delicate hands,
Let others possess what they will
Of learning, and houses, and lands;
My parlor that's next to the sky
I'd quit her blessed mansion to share;
So happy to live and to die
In Dyott-street, Bloomsbury square.

And, oh, would this damsel be mine,
No other provision I'd seek;
On a *look* I could breakfast and dine,
And feast on a *smile* for a week.
But ah! should she false-hearted prove,
Suspended, I'll dangle in air;
A victim to delicate love,
In Dyott-street, Bloomsbury square. [*Exit*, L.

Enter BOMBASTES,* *preceded by a Fifer, playing* "*Michael Wiggins.*"

Bom. Gentle musician, let thy dulcet strain
Proceed—play Michael Wiggins once again,—
Music's the food of love; give o'er, give o'er,
For I must batten on that food no more. [*Exit Fifer*
My happiness is changed to doleful dumps,
Whilst, merry Michael, all thy cards were trumps.
So, should some youth, by fortune's blest decrees,
Possess at least a pound of Cheshire cheese,

* The remainder of the part of Bombastes is usually performed in a morning gown and slippers.

And bent some favored party to regale,
Lay in a kilderkin or so of ale;
Lo! angry fate, in one unlucky hour,
Some hungry rats may all the cheese devour,
And the loud thunder turn the liquor sour.

[*Forms his sash into a noose.*

Alas! alack! alack! and well-a-day,
That ever man should make himself away;
That ever man for woman false should die,
As many have, and so, and so—won't I;
No, I'll go mad! 'gainst all I'll vent my rage,
And with this wicked wanton world a woful war I'll wage.

[*Hangs his boots to the arm of a tree, and taking a scrap of paper, with a pencil writes the following couplet, which he attaches to them, repeating the words.*

"Who dares this pair of boots displace,
Must meet Bombastes face to face."
Thus do I challenge all the human race.

[*Draws his sword and retires up the Stage.*

Enter ARTAXOMINOUS, L.

Art. Scorning my proffered hand he frowning fled,
Cursed the fair maid, and shook his angry head.

[*Perceives the boots and label.*

"Who dares this pair of boots displace,
Must meet Bombastes face to face."
Ha! dost thou dare me, vile obnoxious elf;
I'll make thy threats as *bootless* as thyself;
Where'er thou art, with speed prepare to go
Where I shall send thee—to the shades below!

[*Knocks down the boots.*

Bom. [*Coming forward.*] So have I heard on Afric's burning shore
A hungry lion give a grievous roar;
The grievous roar echoed along the shore.

Art. So have I heard on Afric's burning shore
Another lion give a grievous roar,
And the first lion thought the last a bore.

Bom. Am I then mocked? Now by my fame I swear
You shall have it—There! [*They fight*

Art. Where?

Bom. There, and there.

Art. I have it, sure enough—Oh; I am slain;
I'd give a pot of beer to live again:
Yet, ere I die, I something have to say:
My once loved Gen'ral, prithee, come this way!
Oh! oh! my Bom— [*Falls on his back.*

Bom. —bastes he would have said;
But ere the word was out his breath was fled.
Well, peace be with him, his untimely doom
Shall be thus marked upon his costly tomb:
"Fate cropped him short—for, be it understood,
"He would have lived much longer—if he could."
[*Retires again up the stage*

Enter FUSBOS, L.

Fus. This was the way they came, and much I fear,
There's mischief in the wind—what have we here?
King Artaxominous bereft of life!
Here'll be a pretty tale to tell his wife.

Bom. A pretty tale, but not for thee to tell,
For thou shalt quickly follow him to hell;
There say I sent thee, and I hope he's well.

Fus. No, thou thyself shalt thy own message bear;
Short is the journey, thou wilt soon be there. [*They fight*

* DUET.

AIR—"*Weippert's Fancy.*"

Bom. I'll quickly run you through.
Fus. No, hang me, if you do!
I think I know a trick can equal two of that;
My sword I well can use,
So mind your P's and Q s.
Bom. I thank you, sir; but I must caution you of that

AIR—"*Lord Cathcart's Favorite.*"

Fus. 'Tis a pleasure to fight
With a man so polite,
Then hear in return what I'll do, sir;
I'll take down aught you'll say
In the will-making way,
And be your executor, too, sir.

* This duet is sometimes omitted

Bom. Oh, sir, there's no need
For so friendly a deed,
But I hope for yourself you're provided;
Since your worldly affairs
Will devolve to your heirs,
As soon as the point is decided,
Then come on while you can,
Meet your fate like a man—
Bombastes shall ne'er be derided.

Bom. Oh, Fusbos, Fusbos, I am diddled quite,
Dark clouds come o'er my eyes, farewell, good night!
Good night, my cock, my soul's inclined to roam,
So make my compliments to all at home.
[*Lies down by the King*

Fus. And o'er thy grave a monument shall rise,
Where heroes yet unborn shall feast their eyes;
And this short epitaph that speaks thy fame,
Shall also there immortalize my name:
" Here lies Bombastes, stout of heart and limb,
Who conquered all but Fusbos—Fusbos him."

Enter DISTAFFINA, L.

Dis. Ah, wretched maid! oh, miserab e fate!
I've just arrived in time to be too late;
What now shall hapless Distaffina do?
Curse on all morning dreams, they come so true.

Fus. Go, beauty, go, thou source of wo to man,
And get another lover where you can:
The crown now sits on Griskinissa's head;
To her I'll go—

Dis. But are you sure they're dead?

Fus. Yes, dead as herrings—herrings that are red.

FINALE.

Dis. Briny tears I'll shed.
Art. [*Rising.*] I for joy shall cry, too:
Fus. Zounds! the King's alive;
Bom [*Rising.*] Yes, and so am I too.

Dis. It was better far
Art. Thus to check all sorrow;

Fus. But, if some folks please,
Bom We'll die again to-morrow.

Dis. Tu ral, lu ral, la,
Art. Tu ral, lu ral, laddi;
Fus. Tu ral, lu ral, la,
Bom. Tu ral, lu ral, laddi.

[*They take hands and dance round repeating Chorus.*

THE END.